"It's a different feeling playing for your country [in the Olympics]. When you're playing in the NBA you're playing for a particular city, but when you're playing for your country those lines go away. It carries a great honor that goes above and beyond winning the NBA Championship."

Kobe Bryant

1978–2020

Essential Library

An Imprint of Abdo Publishing | abdobooks.com

KOBE BRYANT

BASKETBALL SUPERSTAR

BY TAMMY GAGNE

CREDITS

abdobooks.com

Published by Abdo Publishing, a division of ABDO, PO Box 398166, Minneapolis, Minnesota 55439. Copyright © 2021 by Abdo Consulting Group, Inc. International copyrights reserved in all countries. No part of this book may be reproduced in any form without written permission from the publisher. Essential Library™ is a trademark and logo of Abdo Publishing.

Printed in the United States of America, North Mankato, Minnesota.
082020
092020

**THIS BOOK CONTAINS
RECYCLED MATERIALS**

Cover Photo: Mark J. Terrill/AP Images
Interior Photos: Mark J. Terrill/AP Images, 1, 60, 78, 84; Douglas C. Pizac/AP Images, 7; Nick Wass/AP Images, 10; Shutterstock Images, 14, 55, 68, 83; Roman Babakin/iStockphoto, 17; Al Messerschmidt/AP Images, 19, 43; Branimir Kvartuc/AP Images, 23; iStockphoto, 24; Gary Hershorn/Reuters/Newscom, 27; Eileen Blass/USA TODAY, 29; Chris Szagola/AP Images, 30; Rusty Kennedy/AP Images, 34; Steve W Grayson UPI Photo Service/Newscom, 37; Elise Amendola/AP Images, 38; Susan Sterner/AP Images, 41, 96; Michael Caulfield/AP Images, 47, 97 (top); Eric Gay/AP Images, 48, 71, 72, 99 (top left); S. Bukley/Shutterstock Images, 52; Hector Mata/AP Images, 57; Matt A. Brown/AP Images, 63, 97 (bottom); Jim Ruymen/UPI/Newscom, 64; Ric Francis/AP Images, 67; Rick Bowmer/AP Images, 77, 99 (top right); Allen Berezovsky/Getty Images Entertainment/Getty Images, 87, 99 (bottom left); Tinseltown/Shutterstock Images, 88; Dylan Stewart/Image of Sport/Newscom, 91; Kelvin Kuo/AP Images, 95, 99 (bottom right)

Editor: Alyssa Krekelberg
Series Designer: Becky Daum

Library of Congress Control Number: 2020932466
Publisher's Cataloging-in-Publication Data
Names: Gagne, Tammy, author.
Title: Kobe Bryant: basketball superstar / by Tammy Gagne
Other title: basketball superstar
Description: Minneapolis, Minnesota : Abdo Publishing, 2021 | Series: Lives cut short
| Includes online resources and index
Identifiers: ISBN 9781532193989 (lib. bdg.) | ISBN 9781098212797 (ebook)
Subjects: LCSH: Bryant, Kobe, 1978-2020--Juvenile literature. | Basketball
players--United States--Biography--Juvenile literature. | Guards (Basketball)--
Biography--Juvenile literature. | Professional athletes--United States--Biography--
Juvenile literature. | African American athletes--Biography--Juvenile literature.
Classification: DDC 796.323092--dc23

 TABLE OF CONTENTS

1

A CAREER-CHANGING GAME

t wasn't the moment that Kobe Bryant had dreamed about for years. Instead, it felt like a nightmare. He was nearing the end of his rookie season with the Los Angeles Lakers. Numerous sportswriters had labeled Bryant as a player to watch. Now was his chance to shine as one of the National Basketball Association's (NBA's) youngest players. The Lakers were up against the Utah Jazz in the 1997 Western Conference semifinals. They were down three games to one in the best-of-seven series.

Losing this one would mean leaving their shot at the championship on the floor in Salt Lake City, Utah.

Several of Bryant's more experienced teammates had been taken out of the game in one way or another. Veteran shooting guard Byron Scott missed the game with a sprained right wrist. Forward Robert Horry was ejected during the third quarter after a scuffle with Utah's Jeff Hornacek. And star Lakers center Shaquille O'Neal had just fouled out with less than two minutes left in the game. The Lakers were counting on 18-year-old Bryant. He was their last hope to win the game and keep the series alive.

So far, the game had been close. This was despite the best efforts of Jazz stars Karl Malone and John Stockton, who together racked up 56 points by the time of the final buzzer. With the score tied 89–89, the game headed into overtime. Bryant scrambled to take every

Working and Waiting for His Turn

Most NBA rookies spend lots of time sitting on the bench. Although Bryant showed great potential, he too had to wait for his chance at floor time. More often than not, Lakers coach Del Harris chose established guards Eddie Jones and Nick Van Exel over Bryant. When Bryant did make it into a game, he often had only a few minutes to prove his value to the team. At the time, Bryant hated being a benchwarmer. But he later said it inspired him to work as hard as he could during practices so he could get more opportunities to get in the game.

jump shot. The impromptu practice session was not an isolated incident meant to blow off steam. It was Bryant's way to make sure that he never repeated the mistakes he made in that fateful game. He kept working on his jump shot every single day until the next NBA season began.

While others may have succumbed to negativity and self-doubt after a big disappointment, Bryant made hard work and perseverance the driving forces that would make him the player he wanted to be. Years later, he recalled that semifinals loss as a turning point in his career. Although it was miserable to go through, Bryant said that he looked back upon that game with fond memories because it helped shape him as a player.

BECOMING THE BLACK MAMBA

As many athletes—both amateur and professional—know, every sport is partly a mental

No Fear

The media quickly began poking fun at Bryant for his four air balls in the 1997 semifinals game. The next day, even the *Los Angeles Times* ran the headline "Lakers Get Aired Out."[2] Soon, however, the conversation shifted. People began to see that Bryant's willingness to keep taking shots despite airballing several was an admirable trait. Former Lakers guard Jerry West was the team's general manager during Bryant's rookie season. West said in an interview about that game with the *Los Angeles Daily News* that Bryant never gave up, even after he faced failure. "He was fearless. I think that's one of the things that spurred him to greatness," said West.[3]

game. A player can have enormous natural talent and highly developed skills, but without a clear vision of what needs to be done in the game, victory can remain out of reach. Professional basketball often requires split-second decisions and aggressive action. Some professional athletes are the nicest, most easygoing people one will ever meet, but when the game clock starts ticking, they seem to become someone else. This was the approach Bryant soon decided to use toward basketball. He even adopted a name for his new, more serious alter ego. He nicknamed himself the Black Mamba, an image that depicted the ferocious attitude he now displayed when he donned

The Origin of the Black Mamba

Bryant got the idea for his Black Mamba nickname while watching director Quentin Tarantino's movie *Kill Bill*. An assassin in the film goes by the code name Black Mamba after using this kind of snake to kill another character. Bryant immediately noticed the similarities between the traits the snake displayed and the qualities he needed to develop on the basketball court. He began researching the black mamba snake species. He soon realized that Tarantino had chosen it because of its reputation as one of the fastest and deadliest snakes in the world. The black mamba's bite is so lethal that it can kill a human being with just two drops of venom. The snake is agile, deadly, and offers no apologies for its actions—exactly how Bryant wanted to be on the basketball court. By becoming the Black Mamba, Bryant could use these killer instincts to defeat his opponents in the NBA.

his purple-and-gold Lakers jersey. Like the deadly snake of the same name, Bryant wasn't going to let anything get in his way.

The nickname quickly caught on with both fans and sportscasters, who watched Bryant morph into the Black Mamba whenever he took the court. People who knew him best understood that neither the moniker nor the mentality that accompanied it had anything to do with who Bryant was in his personal life. When he wasn't playing basketball, he was the same husband, father, son, and friend he had always been. But in basketball, he strove to become the most ruthless player in the game.

During a 2014 interview with the *New Yorker*, Bryant compared his identification as the Black Mamba to the fictional character Bruce Banner and his superhero alter ego, the Incredible Hulk. While Banner and Hulk may share a single body, they are two drastically different beings. A year later, Bryant told sportscaster Ahmad

Doing His Homework

Lakers coach Del Harris noticed that Bryant took his job as an NBA player seriously. Most professional players put lots of time and effort in at practices, but Bryant stayed focused on the game even while others turned to rest and recreation. On the plane rides to and from their games, for example, Harris noticed that Bryant did not play cards or video games to pass the time as others did. Instead, he watched videos of previous Lakers games so he could learn from them.

▲ BRYANT'S WEIGHTY LEGACY WILL STICK WITH BASKETBALL FANS FOR YEARS.

Rashad that his Black Mamba persona allowed him to become "stone cold" on the basketball court.[4] Becoming the Black Mamba allowed Bryant to come through for his team when it mattered most and the pressure was the highest.

Bryant's impressive talent and fierce competitiveness helped propel him to the top of his sport. His 20-year career was among the most successful in NBA history. Even after he retired from professional basketball in 2016, he remained relevant to the sport by passing on his knowledge to up-and-coming basketball stars through his Mamba Sports Academy. Bryant's life came to a tragic end in 2020 when he was killed in a helicopter accident in California. But his strong spirit, his family, and his many fans help his legend endure.

2

KOBE'S
YOUNGER YEARS

obe Bean Bryant was born the first and only son of Joe and Pamela Bryant on August 23, 1978, in Philadelphia, Pennsylvania. The baby's middle name was a nod to his father's NBA nickname, Jelly Bean. Joe made his living as a forward for the Philadelphia 76ers. He had entered the NBA Draft in 1975 after attending Philadelphia's La Salle University. He spent the next four years playing for the 76ers as he and Pamela raised their young children. Kobe's arrival made the Bryants a family of five, as the

couple already had two young daughters, Sharia and Shaya.

Basketball seemed to run through Kobe's blood. His maternal uncle, John "Chubby" Cox, also played briefly in the NBA as a shooting guard for the Washington Bullets.

Joe's career took the Bryants to San Diego, California, when he was traded to the Clippers in 1979. Living in sunny Southern California, Kobe spent plenty of time playing outdoors as a young child. His favorite pastime was playing basketball. Even then, he was envisioning his future in the game. When people asked him what he wanted to be when he grew up, Kobe proudly told them he was going to become an NBA player one day. He idolized Magic Johnson, the star point guard of the Los Angeles Lakers. The team quickly became his favorite.

The Bryant family remained in San Diego for three years. Then Joe moved them again to play for the

Named After Kobe Beef

Joe and Pam Bryant named their son after a famous brand of beef from Japan. Joe had fallen in love with the food as soon as he first tasted it. When Kobe became a professional basketball player, his fame actually propelled the beef company to even greater notoriety throughout the world. Tetsunori Tanimoto, the director of the Kobe Beef Marketing and Distribution Promotion Association, actually credits the basketball star with cementing the brand in people's minds as such a valuable commodity.

▲ MAGIC JOHNSON WAS THE FACE OF THE LAKERS THROUGH THE 1980S.

Houston Rockets. His single season with that team would bring his eight-year NBA career to a close.

GROWING UP IN EUROPE

When the Rockets chose not to renew Joe's contract, he made a big decision. He signed with a basketball team in central Italy. The Bryant family was on the move again. Kobe and his siblings were excited for the new adventure that awaited them in Europe, but they also knew that some parts of it would be hard, at least at first. Kobe was just six years old, and neither he nor his sisters spoke any Italian. When they first arrived in the foreign country, the children began spending a lot of time together. This led them to become incredibly close. Together, they constantly practiced Italian words and phrases so they could better communicate with other people their age.

The longer they lived there, the more their social circle expanded. In addition to their new Italian friends, the Bryant kids

Perfect Italian

Having spent several years of his childhood in Italy, Kobe became fluent in Italian. During a 2011 interview with a popular radio station back in Italy, he sounded like he had never returned to the United States from his European home. He spoke perfect Italian when he said, "I grew up here in Italy, it's a country that will always be close to my heart. Always."[1]

also befriended the sons and daughters of the other American players on their father's team. Among them was Tamika Catchings, who would later play in the Women's National Basketball Association (WNBA). Sharia and Shaya Bryant were also athletic children, but their brother's love for basketball bordered on obsession. When he was just a kindergartner, Kobe would often sneak out of his family's home to shoot baskets at a nearby church playground. His new life in Italy had turned out pretty well.

Time to Play

As a professional basketball player in Italy, Joe Bryant regularly attended practices with his teammates. Kobe would often tag along on these trips to the gymnasium. His father's former teammates still remember the young boy who played his own games while he was there. Antonio Olivieri was one of those teammates. He has said that all the players had to keep an eye on the boy, as he would actually climb into the hoops while they played.

Joe also shined in his new setting. He quickly became a star on the Italian basketball court, often scoring 30 to 40 points per game. The fans loved him, and they made the whole Bryant family feel like welcome additions to the central Italian city of Rieti. Sometimes young Kobe would even entertain the crowds by shooting baskets at halftime. He continued playing the sport himself, often practicing alongside his father. He studied his dad's moves carefully, learning as much as he could about the game.

Kobe also enjoyed playing soccer. His Italian friends urged him to play the popular game, sure that his long arms and speed would make him an ideal goalie. Still, basketball remained Kobe's favorite pastime. He even continued to follow the NBA from a continent away. His grandparents, who still lived in the United States, recorded games and mailed the VHS tapes to him each week.

Joe ended up playing for more

Lifetime Impressions

Kobe remained close with the friends he made in Italy for the rest of his life. Although they no longer resided in the same country as adults, Kobe visited whenever his busy schedule allowed. His time in Italy had played an important role in the person and the professional player that he became many years later. He and friends from this era would catch up as often as they could. They also continued to laugh at and goad one another in a lighthearted manner every chance they got. The joking was always good-natured fun. One of these friends was Davide Giudici, who last saw Kobe shortly after Kobe retired from the NBA. At this time, Giudici teased his longtime friend by telling him that *he* was still playing basketball—in a small Italian league—even if Kobe wasn't still playing the game himself. Giudici shared this story with NBC News in 2020, admitting to the reporter something that he left out when he had teased his friend. "When he moved to Reggio Emilia [as a kid] and started playing in my team, it was immediately clear he was from another planet, a cut above us all," Giudici said.[2]

▲ KOBE AND HIS FATHER LAUGH TOGETHER BEFORE A
PICKUP GAME IN 2007.

than one team in Italy, just like many NBA
players do in the United States. After Rieti, the
family ended up moving to three other Italian
cities: Reggio Calabria in the south, a Tuscan city
named Cireglio, and lastly—by the time Kobe
was 12—Reggio Emilia in northern Italy.

▲ TO GET BETTER AT BASKETBALL, PEOPLE NEED TO PRACTICE BOTH ALONE AND WITH OTHERS.

A SERIOUS GAME

Kobe joined a youth team in Reggio Emilia. To most other kids his age, basketball was just a fun after-school activity, but to Kobe, it was so much more. He put in more effort than anyone else on his team. After a game or a practice, his teammates would move on to take part in the less demanding activities that most kids their age enjoyed. While they headed to the movies or home to watch television, though, Kobe headed to the garden behind his house, where his father had installed a basketball hoop.

He told his Italian friends that he was going to become a professional basketball player one day. Despite Kobe's seriousness, his pals responded the way many kids do when imagining such a lofty ambition—they laughed. To them, it was as if he were saying he was going to become an astronaut or a rock star. Their disbelief did not dissuade Kobe, though. As hard as he knew it would be, he also knew a professional basketball career was possible. He had seen his father accomplish the feat, and he hoped that he had inherited some of Joe's talent for the game. Kobe was willing to give it everything he had.

3

BACK IN THE USA

When Joe Bryant's professional basketball career came to an end in 1991, the family returned to the United States. They headed straight for the city that had been their home when Kobe was born—Philadelphia. Joe took a job as a high school basketball coach at Akiba Hebrew Academy in nearby Bryn Mawr, and Kobe no longer had to wait for family members to send VHS tapes of NBA games to him overseas. He could now watch them on television in real time.

▸ DURING HIS NBA CAREER, KOBE WAS ABLE TO GO HEAD-TO-HEAD WITH PLAYERS HE HAD GROWN UP ADMIRING, SUCH AS MICHAEL JORDAN.

Although Kobe still followed the 76ers and the Lakers, he had a new idol—a driven and competitive Chicago Bulls player named Michael Jordan. Kobe had first seen Jordan on videotape back in Italy. Now he began looking to Jordan as the best example of the player and leader he wanted to become.

Kobe wasn't the only one who had high expectations for his future. Local fans who had followed Joe's NBA career were excited to see him return to the United States with his family. The *Philadelphia Inquirer* even reported that Bryant had enrolled his kids in Lower Merion Township school district, printing a prediction that they would provide a boost to the school's basketball team.

A MIDDLE SCHOOL STANDOUT

Kobe was just 13 when he started playing basketball in Philly. His skills attracted the attention of coaches at the high school level. One of them was Gregg Downer, who coached the Lower Merion High School Aces. He went to see one of Kobe's games after hearing how talented the middle school guard was. Unfortunately, Kobe spent much of that game on the bench, but not because he wasn't helping his team succeed. The middle school team had a rule that required

▲ KOBE WAS A STAR PLAYER ON THE LOWER MERION HIGH SCHOOL ACES IN 1995.

▲ AFTER KOBE SKYROCKETED TO FAME, HIS HIGH SCHOOL NAMED ITS GYMNASIUM AFTER HIM. PEOPLE LEFT FLOWERS FOR KOBE OUTSIDE THE GYM AFTER HIS DEATH.

every player to pass the ball a certain number of times. Kobe was focused on winning the game, not passing the ball to satisfy a quota. For this reason the coach kept pulling him off the court.

Downer had seen enough, however, to know that Kobe's skills far exceeded those of the other players on the team. He extended an invitation for Kobe to practice with his high school varsity team. Downer figured that it was the only way he would be able to see what the kid could really do. Just minutes into the practice, Downer told his assistant coaches that they were looking at a future pro.

STAR PLAYER OF THE LOWER MERION ACES

The following year, Kobe entered Lower Merion High School and joined its basketball team. Although he was only a freshman, he made the varsity team and quickly became a starting player. Despite Kobe's best efforts on the court,

Learning More than Basketball

Basketball wasn't the only thing Kobe enjoyed while he was a student at Lower Merion High School. He was also a good student. One of his favorite instructors was an English teacher named Jeanne Mastriano. Kobe took his first class with her during his sophomore year at the school, then another when he was a senior. Mastriano introduced Kobe to mythology, which he remembered through the years with great affection. He even spoke about the influence that myths about heroes' journeys had on him during media interviews as a professional player. He and Mastriano kept in touch after he graduated and throughout Kobe's entire career. He said that she opened his eyes to the power of storytelling. He often visited the school on trips back to his hometown, but no matter how much Mastriano insisted that Kobe could now call her by her first name, he refused. To him, he explained to her, she would always be Mrs. Mastriano, his teacher.

though, the Aces won just four games during the whole season. Knowing he had the ability to accomplish so much more, Kobe dedicated himself to that task. When he was in class, Kobe focused on the work at hand and earned good grades. But when it was time for basketball, he was entirely present in that moment. Jeremy Treatman, who was an assistant coach at Lower Merion High School at the time, remembered that Kobe was so invested in his sport that he became upset if the school had to cancel a practice. He had a clear vision of his goals, and he placed himself firmly on the path to achieving them.

Kobe spent much of the summer practicing his skills. Feeling confident, he challenged his father to a one-on-one game. The younger Bryant soon realized that he still had a lot of work to do before he could beat his more experienced father, though. In the beginning Kobe grabbed the

A Prize-Winning Shot

When Kobe's high school class went on a field trip to a nearby amusement park, one of his friends—a girl named Susan—asked whether he would try to win her a giant blue elephant at one of the carnival-style basketball games. These games are designed to be nearly impossible to win, but nothing seemed impossible when Kobe had a basketball. After winning his friend the elephant, which was bigger than she was, Kobe asked to play again. According to Susan's mother, who shared the story with USA Today, the park employee responded by telling him to get lost.

ball and made it past his older opponent. The teen assumed that his youth and agility would lead him to an overall victory, but then Joe surprised his son by getting past him and swiftly sinking the ball into the net. Kobe later told the *Philadelphia Inquirer* that he hadn't realized just how fast his father still was.

Kobe's hard work was starting to pay off. During his sophomore season with the Aces, he averaged 22 points and ten rebounds per game, but even these numbers were not enough to take the team much further than the previous year. As a junior, however, Kobe proved that he could be the kind of leader he had dreamed of being. He helped the Aces win their first Central League championship in two decades. Kobe scored 42 points in one game, his personal best at that time. Although the team lost in the second round of the state playoffs, people throughout Pennsylvania—and beyond— were talking about the young man whose basketball skills ran as deep as his love for the

A Strong Work Ethic

Kobe's high school coach described him as a charismatic young man with plenty of personality, but when it came to the game, his coach said that Kobe was all business. Kobe was always the first player to show up for practice, and he was reliably the last one to leave the court hours later. He would even go to the gym on snow days. If it had to do with basketball, Kobe didn't joke around.

▲ KOBE DUNKS A BALL DURING A 1996 PRACTICE.

game. The *Philadelphia Inquirer* named Kobe the all-area player of the year.

A BIG DECISION

The only thing left for Kobe to do before graduating from high school was to finally snag that elusive state championship. That is just what he and his fellow Aces did during Kobe's final year at Lower Merion. In a 48–43 win over Erie Cathedral Prep, the Aces won their first Class AAAA title since 1943.

While Kobe's classmates were deciding which universities to apply to and worrying about whether they would be accepted, Kobe was grappling with a different decision: Should he go to college or declare himself eligible for the NBA Draft? He had continued to excel academically through high school, and his SAT scores were high, but college was not his only option. Coaches were assuring him that he was good enough to go straight into the pros.

Learning from the Pros

Kobe started working out with the Philadelphia 76ers while he was still in high school. Although the arrangement definitely worked in his favor, it was not completely one-sided. Head coach and general manager John Lucas used the talented high schooler to test other players. He would bring in draft prospects and have them go one-on-one against Kobe. Those who could hold their own against Kobe stayed on the coach's short list of players who had the potential to make it into the NBA.

4

GOING PRO

By the time Bryant was preparing to graduate from Lower Merion High School in 1996, he had already made a name for himself in basketball. *USA Today* even named him its high school player of the year. The 17-year-old sensation had broken all the high school scoring records that Wilt Chamberlain had set in southern Pennsylvania more than 40 years earlier. Like Bryant, Chamberlain had numerous offers to play at the college level. More than 100 universities

▶ IN 1996, SOME NBA TEAMS BELIEVED BRYANT WAS READY TO GO PRO.

▲ KEVIN GARNETT, *LEFT*, WAS ONE OF BASKETBALL'S GREATS. HIS ATHLETICISM, SIZE, AND SHOOTING SKILLS MADE HIM A DIFFICULT OPPONENT TO FACE.

pursued him.[1] But Bryant was seriously considering skipping college ball altogether.

Forgoing college basketball to enter the NBA Draft was almost unheard of at this time. One year earlier, in 1995, Kevin Garnett went straight from high school to the pros. However, before Garnett no player had made that leap in 20 years. And there was one big difference between Garnett and Bryant: their size. Garnett, who stood nearly seven feet tall, was a power forward who already matched up well with other NBA forwards. All of the other players who had made the jump from high school to the pros had been similarly big players. Bryant, meanwhile, stood six-foot-six and wasn't as physically developed as other NBA guards.

GOING FOR IT

Bryant was confident that he would be claimed in the NBA Draft. He believed that his natural talent for the game combined with his proven ability on the basketball court would lead him to the professional career he had been dreaming of since he was a child. *Philadelphia Inquirer* sportswriter Bob Ford was just one of many people who thought that 76ers head coach and general manager John Lucas would snag Bryant with the team's first overall pick. But Lucas was fired just a little over a month before the draft took place in 1996. The 76ers selected Georgetown University point guard Allen Iverson in the draft instead of Bryant.

As most basketball fans know, draft picks are frequently the subject of bartering. Teams often trade picks with one another in an attempt to end up in a better position down the road. They will also trade newly selected players after picking them. This ended up being the case for Bryant, who was initially chosen by the Charlotte Hornets

Small Doubts

Even as a teenager, Bryant always projected confidence. He wasn't afraid of making big decisions on or off the court, but this doesn't mean he never questioned his own judgment. Entering the NBA Draft was a bold choice for Bryant in 1996. As certain as he seemed about the decision, he had some doubts at first about whether he had made the right choice. As he moved into the enviable position of donning a Lakers jersey, he was watching many of his friends from high school doing something he wasn't: playing in actual games. His peers who chose to play college ball first were getting to do what they all loved most while Bryant was spending most of his time sitting on a bench watching others. "I saw my peers playing 30–35 minutes per game doing their thing, and I am sitting here glued to the bench," Bryant recalled during a podcast interview. "That was the hardest part."[2] For a while he was convinced that he should have tried the more traditional path to the pros. He was an NBA player now, but waiting for his chance to shine was proving to be more difficult than he'd imagined it would be.

▲ BRYANT KNEW THE HORNETS DIDN'T REALLY WANT HIM.
SO HE WAS EXCITED TO BE TRADED TO THE LAKERS.

Before Bryant had even played his first NBA game, he was appearing on national television. People seemed to know that this young man from Philadelphia was going to become a big name in basketball. He was featured on *The Tonight Show*, as well as on popular sitcoms such as *Moesha* and *Sister, Sister*. He even appeared in a sneaker commercial for Adidas. A year later, the company created a signature shoe in his honor—the KB8, also known as the Crazy 8.

with the thirteenth overall pick. Selecting Bryant had been part of Charlotte's plan to get Lakers center Vlade Divac. Within days of the June 26 draft, the teams made a one-for-one trade. Divac went to Charlotte, and Bryant was officially a member of the Los Angeles Lakers, the team he had revered since living in Southern California so many years ago. He was also one of the youngest players in Lakers' history.

HIS CHANCE TO SHINE

Getting traded to the Lakers was the best thing that could have happened to Bryant in more ways than one. As Bryant confirmed to the media years later, Hornets coach Dave Cowens had never planned to use Bryant on his team. The risk Cowens had taken in choosing the young basketball prodigy was in hoping the Lakers would want him badly enough to trade the more experienced Divac for him. Charlotte had no real need for Bryant; the team already had several players on its roster who filled its needs for guards

▲ VLADE DIVAC HAD BEEN WITH THE LAKERS SINCE 1989 BEFORE BEING TRADED TO THE HORNETS.

and small forwards, the positions that Bryant excelled at playing. Even if the Hornets kept him, the arrangement would have been a lackluster one for Bryant, who was sure to spend more than his share of time watching games from the bench while his more seasoned teammates took care of business.

With the Lakers, Bryant had a real shot at playing the game he loved so much. He signed a $3.5 million deal for three years with the Los Angeles team—with a little help from his mother and father.[3] Bryant, who was still 17 at the time, needed his parents to cosign the deal. In return for this big investment in him, Bryant knew that he now had to show the Lakers that he was worth the chance that the team had taken.

The Shot He Needed

It seemed that all Bryant needed to prove himself as a valuable member of the Los Angeles Lakers was just a few more minutes of court time. Two days after his NBA debut, he took to the court again, this time scoring for his team with a free throw in a game against the New York Knicks. Although Bryant still hadn't shown his coaches all he was capable of, he did earn his first NBA point.

A SLOW START

On November 3, 1996, Bryant left the bench for the first time in his NBA career. He played just six minutes in a game against the Minnesota Timberwolves. He had a rebound, a block, and a steal, but he did not score any points for his new team.

Instead, another new Laker named Shaquille O'Neal stole the show, scoring 35 points for Los Angeles. The Lakers won the game 91–85 with little help from Bryant.

Soon, Bryant would show his coaches that he deserved more playing time. In his fourth appearance on the court, he scored double digits for the first time. On January 3, he scored 21 points in a victory over the Sacramento Kings. By the end of the season, Bryant's season high was 24 points in 25 minutes of play against the Golden State Warriors on April 8. It was becoming obvious what Bryant could bring to his new team.

All-Rookie Honors

In the 1996–97 season, Bryant was named to the All-Rookie Second Team, an undeniable honor for the youngest player in the NBA. Still, when his fans look back at this time in his life, some might find it surprising that the future great was only a second-team choice. In a sense it shows how much Bryant grew as a player during his early years in the NBA.

5

Early Challenges, Fame, and Family

Lakers head coach Del Harris hoped that Bryant and center Shaquille O'Neal would mesh well when they joined the team for the 1996–97 season. The team's success relied heavily on the pair's ability to work well under pressure. Unfortunately, this was not an easy task in the beginning. Although Bryant and Shaq—as O'Neal was known—played for the same team, they also saw each other as rivals to a degree. As Shaq explained years later, it was never about a dislike of each other. Rather, each player wanted

▶ Bryant takes a shot during a summer league game with the Lakers in July 1996.

▲ BRYANT AND SHAQ WORKED TOGETHER TO WIN GAMES FOR THE LAKERS.

to be the star of the Lakers. In some ways this rivalry was a healthy one; their competition helped push each of them to succeed. But in other ways, it held them back from working cohesively as team members. Having a good coach can make all the difference in a situation like this one. Harris, and later Phil Jackson, helped the two men focus all their energy on winning games instead of competing with each other.

This change did not happen overnight, but the players gradually came to respect each other's abilities. Six years older than Bryant, Shaq had hoped to serve as a big brother of sorts to the younger player when they both joined the team. He had already played four seasons with the Orlando Magic before coming to Los Angeles, and he had wisdom to impart from the experience. Bryant, however, was not looking for another mentor. He wanted to be seen as an equal, and he was willing to work hard to prove that he was worthy of that distinction. The only way the two players could prove their true worth was by overcoming their egos to help each other on the court.

As the two learned to combine their skills to crush their opponents instead of trying to one-up each other, Bryant and Shaq began leading their team to victory after victory. The Lakers won three NBA championships in a row between June 2000 and June 2002, ending a 12-year title drought. In the final game of the 2000 NBA Finals against the Indiana Pacers, the pair combined for 67 points in the Lakers' 116–111 victory, proving once and for all it was better to work together than separately.

FINDING HAPPINESS OFF THE COURT

As Bryant's NBA career was taking off, he was also dabbling in a side career in rap music. He had long been a fan of hip-hop. Now he wanted to see whether he could become a rap artist himself. In 1999, Bryant recorded an album with Sony Records called *K.O.B.E.*, but the endeavor was far from a successful one. Both professional critics and friends discouraged Bryant from taking the venture any further. Rapper LL Cool J, who had become a buddy of Bryant's, told him in private that he should stick with basketball.

Standing Out

By Bryant's second NBA season, he was becoming more comfortable in his role as a Laker. He was also proving how capable he was on any court. Bryant became the youngest starter in the NBA All-Star game that year, but he was determined to become an even better player. In February 2002, he was named the All-Star most valuable player (MVP). It was the first of four times he would earn this title in his career.

Years later, they would laugh about the conversation. But the album wasn't a waste of time. It led Bryant to meet the young woman who would later become his wife.

Vanessa Laine was a senior at Marina High School in Huntington Beach, California, when she met Bryant at a video shoot for one of his rap songs. After being discovered in the audience at a concert, Vanessa had appeared in another rap video previously. Bryant was drawn to her as soon as the two were introduced. He asked for her phone number and soon planned their first date, a trip to Disneyland. It wasn't a typical trip to the amusement park, however. Bryant traveled with bodyguards, and they accompanied the couple throughout the park.

Years later, other former Huntington students recalled the commotion that Bryant caused when the pro basketballer showed up at their high school to pick up Vanessa in his Mercedes-Benz. On several occasions he had huge bouquets of

Something New

Bryant's relationship with Vanessa was different from any other relationships he'd ever had. When describing this time in his life, he later said that she quickly became his best friend. "I had been so used to growing up in isolation, really," he pointed out. "Moving around from place to place, making new friends all the time, so I never really opened up to anybody because I knew I was just going to inevitably move."[1]

▲ BRYANT AND VANESSA GOT ENGAGED AFTER KNOWING EACH OTHER FOR SIX MONTHS.

roses delivered to the school for her. The couple continued dating until Vanessa turned 18. Bryant proposed at her birthday party. They married in 2001 in a small church ceremony in Dana Point, California.

STARTING A FAMILY

On January 19, 2003, the Bryants welcomed their first child, a daughter named Natalia, whom they nicknamed Nani. Their second daughter, Gianna, joined the family on May 1, 2006. Daughter Bianka was born on December 5, 2016, and the baby of the family, Capri, arrived on June 20, 2019. A proud husband and father, Bryant often referred to Vanessa as his queen and their girls as his princesses. Natalia wasn't the only one they gave a nickname. Gianna, Bianka, and Capri respectively became Gigi, BiBi, and KoKo.

Bryant had a special relationship with each of his daughters. He especially enjoyed attending Natalia's volleyball games, in which she played the position of

Italian Names

Bryant's fond memories of his childhood in Italy inspired him and Vanessa to choose Italian names for their daughters. Nani's full name is Natalia Diamante. Natalia means "born on Christmas Day," while *diamante* is the Italian word for "diamond." Gigi's full name was Gianna Maria-Onore. Gianna is the Italian form of Jane. BiBi's middle name, Bella, means "beautiful," and KoKo's full name, Capri, is the name of an Italian island in the Bay of Naples.

middle hitter. Gianna, though, shared his love of basketball. She enjoyed watching the sport with her father, both in person and on television. When she was old enough to play the game competitively, he even coached her teams. The time he spent with his younger daughters was different but just as special to him. In 2019, he said in an interview that one of his favorite things to do was sing Barney songs with them. "I played [basketball for] 20 years and I missed those moments before. For me to make the trip up to Staples Center, that means I'm missing an opportunity to spend another night with my kids when I know how fast it goes. I want to make sure the days that I'm away from them are days that I absolutely have to be. I'd rather be with them than doing anything else."[2]

▲ BRYANT'S FAMILY WAS AN IMPORTANT PART OF HIS LIFE.

6

A CAREER TO BE PROUD OF

As Bryant rose to fame, sportswriters often compared his competitive attitude to that of Michael Jordan, the Chicago Bulls superstar who had long been Bryant's idol. Both players were amazing dunkers. Both also excelled at driving to the hoop. They also both had a great midrange game, although each had his own specialty shots. Many fans will argue that Bryant had by far the better jump shot.

The comparisons between the two pleased Bryant. After all, he had striven to become the

▶ BRYANT ESTABLISHED HIMSELF AS A FORCE ON THE COURT FOR THE LAKERS.

type of player Jordan was. Many fans and experts consider Jordan to be the greatest basketball player of all time. As the Bulls player neared the end of his NBA career, Bryant seemed to be challenging him for this title.

In the late 1990s, Jordan also became much more than an idol to Bryant. What began as Bryant's admiration for the more experienced player grew into a friendship between the two men. Bryant told the press that no one truly understood the impact Jordan had on him as both a player and leader. Jordan generously offered Bryant advice on everything from game strategies to

Comparisons to Other Stars

Part of being a professional basketball player means being continually compared to other NBA players by both the media and fans. For Bryant, this meant being matched against an array of NBA stars over the years. Because he played alongside Shaq for so long, Bryant was often measured against his Lakers teammate. The direction in which the needle tipped usually depended on which one of the pair had performed better on the court in recent games. Other comparisons included those to LeBron James, the star player of the Cleveland Cavaliers, the Miami Heat, and eventually the Lakers. Bryant would also inevitably be likened to Michael Jordan repeatedly. Even though the two players never went up against each other in their respective primes, Jordan and Bryant had much in common. In addition to playing the game with the same ferocity, they both reliably ranked among the best players on an NBA court.

workout regimens. Although there was always a healthy competition between the two players, Jordan chose to mentor Bryant, which meant the world to the young star.

TO STAY OR TO GO?

It isn't unusual for NBA players to play for more than one team during their careers. Some players get traded to other teams. Others accept competing offers after their contracts expire. Bryant, however, had been a Los Angeles Laker since his very first game in the NBA in 1996. He had been the youngest Laker, the rising star, and a proven leader of the team. During this time several other teams tried to acquire Bryant. From the nearby Clippers to the Chicago Bulls, other NBA coaches wanted him.

For years, Bryant hadn't seriously considered the offers. He enjoyed being a Laker, even though it meant sharing the spotlight with Shaq. Together they had learned to lead their team to victory, including the championship "three-peat" from 2000 to 2002. With the massive Shaq

Falling Short

After winning three championships, Bryant and the rest of the Lakers seemed unstoppable. Fans were sure that Los Angeles would continue its streak the following year, but the 2002–03 NBA season proved to be a difficult one for the team. The Lakers got knocked out of the playoffs in the second round. During an interview shortly after the devastating loss, Bryant told the media that he hated the weight of defeat. He said he never wanted to feel it again.

▲ BRYANT AND SHAQ WERE A DOMINANT DUO.

dominating opponents under the basket and
Bryant's lethal shooting skills, their partnership
was nearly unstoppable. But soon some of their
magic began to run out. The Lakers fell short in

the 2003 playoffs, and then a star-studded Lakers team lost in the 2004 NBA Finals. During the latter season, rumors swirled about either Bryant or Shaq being traded.

Bryant knew that he was still capable of greatness. He wanted another NBA championship. He also didn't want people thinking that he could win only with the help of Shaq. Although he thought it was unfair, he knew that some fans had said that Magic Johnson had never won without Kareem Abdul-Jabbar, and that Jordan hadn't won without Scottie Pippen. While Bryant had learned to play as part of a team, he didn't want his success to be seen as reliant on Shaq in this way.

Bryant had tentatively agreed to play for the Bulls when news broke that Shaq had requested a trade. He was joining the Miami Heat. Bryant now had his chance to show the world that he could be as good without his fellow star player

Another Trip to the Finals

Bryant and the Lakers came close to winning another championship in 2004, but they lost in the Finals to the Detroit Pistons. It was another difficult loss for Bryant, one that some sportswriters suspected was his biggest regret at the end of his career. Years later, Bryant said that the loss absolutely still bothered him. He described it as the only time that Detroit's Richard Hamilton had ever beaten him. The two had played against each other in high school too.

as he'd been with him. He would remain with the Lakers after all. Most fans didn't even realize how close Los Angeles had come to losing him to Chicago that year.

A STUNNING GAME

Bryant's career included many exciting games. Some were nail-biters, with the score remaining close right until the end, when the Lakers usually pulled away. Other games were runaways, with the Black Mamba and the Lakers dominating their opponents throughout. A game that stands out to Bryant's biggest fans is one that he played on January 22, 2006. It was against the Toronto Raptors.

Bryant had played more than 1,200 games by this point in his career, but this night would be different in a big way. During the first few minutes of the third quarter, Toronto had racked up an 18-point lead. Then it was like a switch flipped in Bryant. From that point forward, he took over the court. He scored 27 points in just the third quarter. Bryant's command of the court continued as the game entered its final phase, with the Lakers star earning another 28 points

▲ Bryant shoots over a Raptors player in his remarkable 2006 game.

▲ DURING BRYANT'S INTERVIEW AFTER HIS 81-POINT
GAME, THE CROWD BEGAN CHANTING HIS NAME.

in the fourth quarter. In the end, Los Angeles roared back to win 122–104. Even more amazingly, Bryant finished with 81 points.

It was a career high for the already amazing NBA star. Only one other player in the history of the league had scored more points in a single game. Wilt Chamberlain set the record with a 100-point game in 1962. Only four other NBA players had scored more than 70 points in one game.[1] Not even Jordan had scored more than 69—and he reached this number only once. Bryant's fans would talk about this game for years.

The New Leader

After playing alongside Shaq for his entire NBA career up to 2004, Bryant was on the verge of a new era. He was no longer part of a perceived pair on the court. Instead, he was now the unofficial sole leader of the Lakers. The change offered him a new challenge and new hope for solidifying his reputation as one of basketball's greats.

7

MVP Awards and Gold Medals

*E*ach year, NBA writers and broadcasters select one player who stands out among the rest in professional basketball. This player receives the prestigious most valuable player (MVP) award for the regular season. After 12 seasons with the Los Angeles Lakers, though, Bryant had yet to receive the honor. Three former Lakers had won the award. Shaquille O'Neal took it home in 2000, and Magic Johnson won it three times.[1] Kareem Abdul-Jabbar had six MVP awards under his belt.[2] Bryant had been close a few times, coming

▶ Bryant accepts his first MVP award in May 2008.

▲ BRYANT EARNED INTERNATIONAL FAME AND RECOGNITION.

in third, fourth, and fifth place in the voting. But he was never first until the 2007–08 season.

Many of his fans thought the MVP award was long overdue for Bryant. He had proven his abilities on the court repeatedly, but unlike scoring records and championship titles, which are undisputable, voting for the MVP is a more subjective process. Scoring is not the only factor voters consider. They also weigh how well a player leads his team, especially in high-pressure situations.

Still, points matter, and Bryant scored more than his share during this season. He averaged 28.3 points per game, second only to LeBron James, but many experts thought he outperformed James on defense. Although the Lakers ultimately lost the 2008 championship to the Boston Celtics, Bryant was no longer trying to win as a one-man—or even a two-man—team. He was sharing the ball and trusting his teammates, even inspiring them.

Bryant won the MVP award for the 2007–08 season with 82 of 126 first-place votes.[3] Following the announcement, Bryant spoke to the media about the award, pointing out how much it meant to him because it stood for teamwork.

No. 8 and No. 24

Bryant started his NBA career wearing a No. 8 jersey. Although he would have liked to have kept the No. 24 he wore while playing for Lower Merion High School, Lakers forward George McCloud already had that number. Bryant had also played as No. 33 in high school, but the Lakers retired that number in honor of former star Kareem Abdul-Jabbar. Bryant chose No. 8 because it had belonged to him when he played back in Italy. At the start of the 2006–07 season, Bryant decided to again wear No. 24. In addition to its sentimental value, he also saw the higher number as representing his growth as a player. He said it was a way to go back to his roots and evolve at the same time.

"MVP nowadays is not an individual award," Bryant said. "You really have to make your teammates better and elevate your ballclub. For me to be nominated in that race is a tremendous honor because that's really been one of the criticisms that people have had of me, is how well do I make my teammates better. From that standpoint, I feel like I've already won."[4]

BRINGING HOME THE GOLD

By the time 2008 arrived, there were very few things Bryant had not accomplished on a basketball court. But one thing he hadn't done was win an Olympic gold medal. With the 2008 Summer Games around the corner in Beijing, China, Bryant wasn't going to let anything get in his way. When he tore a ligament in one of his fingers shortly before the two-week-long trip, he opted to postpone surgery so he could still compete for Team USA.

The United States had a good shot at bringing home the gold. Beginning in 1992, NBA players were allowed to compete in the Olympics, and Team USA had dominated the men's basketball competition ever since. The so-called Dream Team took gold in 1992, and the Americans won the next two gold medals as well. However, in 2004 they suffered a shocking loss to Argentina

▲ BRYANT FIGHTS FOR THE BALL AGAINST ARGENTINA DURING THE 2008 OLYMPICS.

in the semifinals. The United States settled for the bronze medal that year. Bryant, however, was not part of that team.

In Beijing four years later, the Americans wanted to reclaim the top spot on the podium. Bryant's Olympic dreams were also personal. He wanted to win while playing the best teams in the whole world.

The 2008 US roster—often referred to as the Redeem Team—was filled with NBA All-Stars, including James, Dwyane Wade, Carmelo

▲ BRYANT AND HIS TEAMMATES PROUDLY DISPLAY THEIR
GOLD MEDALS AFTER DEFEATING SPAIN.

Anthony, Dwight Howard, and Chris Paul. Each
of them was used to being the best player on
his team. Winning a gold medal meant putting
egos aside and coming together for a common
cause. And the 29-year-old Bryant was their
undisputed leader.

Team USA cruised through the tournament's
opening round, going 5–0 in pool play and
outscoring their opponents by an average of
32 points per game. Once the medal round
began, Bryant truly took over. He scored an
Olympic career game-high of 25 points in the
116–85 victory over Australia in the quarterfinals.

He chipped in 12 points as Team USA got revenge against Argentina in the semifinals. And in the gold-medal game against Spain, Bryant scored 20 points and had six assists in a 118–107 victory. Bryant had earned his coveted gold medal, and Americans were back on top of the international basketball world.

Bryant went on to win a second gold medal as part of Team USA at the London Olympics in 2012. But that first Olympics in Beijing always carried a special place in his heart.

"It was something that was very personal to us to put our country back on top," Bryant said years later. "It's a different feeling playing for your country. When you're playing in the NBA you're playing for a particular city, but when you're playing for your country those lines go away. It carries a great honor that goes above and beyond winning the NBA Championship."[5]

Another Record

In 2010, Bryant reached an impressive milestone. It related to Jerry West's long-standing record as the all-time highest Lakers scorer. Starting in 1960, West spent 14 seasons with the Lakers, earning 25,192 points for the team during this time span. In February 2010, Bryant surpassed this number during an away game against the Memphis Grizzlies. By the end of the second quarter, Bryant was a mere five points away from tying West's number, but by the end of the third quarter, he had done it—a career total of 25,193.[6] The record was now his.

TWO MORE NBA CHAMPIONSHIPS

Coming off the momentum of the 2008 Olympics, Bryant entered the 2008–09 NBA season determined to retake the title that he and his fellow Lakers had come so close to earning the previous year. Bryant was still an athlete who utilized his losses as fuel to do better next time. He told the press that the Lakers' loss in the 2008 Finals haunted him. When the Celtics won games in that series, the arena played the song "Don't Stop Believin'" by Journey. Boston fans would sing along with it each time. Bryant said he hated the song for two years, but he listened to it every day to remind him of how losing that championship had made him feel.

Bryant had also grown by leaps and bounds from the young man who spent an entire night working on his jump shot all alone as a rookie. Now he was a proven leader, a player who knew how to unite and motivate the rest of his team to join him in the fight for the title they all so deeply wanted. He hadn't lost his killer instinct on the

Finals MVP

Bryant's return to the NBA Finals—and subsequent championship win—earned him the NBA Finals MVP Award in 2009. He averaged 30.2 points per game in the postseason. He received the Finals MVP honor a second time the following year after he led the Lakers to their second consecutive championship in as many years.

court, however. He led by example. Sportswriters noted that he hardly ever smiled during games that season. The Black Mamba was focused on winning his fourth NBA championship.

The title, which the Lakers won after beating the Orlando Magic in the Finals, was a special one for Bryant. Anyone who said that he wasn't good enough to do it without Shaq had finally been proven wrong. Bryant scored 32 points in the fourth game of the series, which often had fans on the edges of their seats. Proving himself a capable leader, Bryant also steered his teammates to match his effort. But just in case anyone still questioned Bryant's abilities, he went on to repeat the accomplishment in June 2010. That time, he and his fellow Lakers beat the Celtics to earn his fifth championship.

Surpassing Jordan

Despite Bryant and Michael Jordan being close friends, a healthy competition always existed between them. Bryant didn't just want to do as well as his idol; he wanted to do even better. Beating Jordan was the highest bar that he could set for himself, and in 2014, he rose above his friend and mentor on the all-time scoring list. Bryant's 32,293rd point, scored during a game against the Minnesota Timberwolves, put him in third place on the list.[7] Only Karl Malone and Kareem Abdul-Jabbar ranked ahead of him.

8

AN ENDING AND A NEW BEGINNING

Every athletic career, no matter how successful or thrilling, must eventually come to an end. The more time that Bryant played professional basketball, the more injuries he experienced. A torn Achilles tendon suffered in April 2013 sidelined him for six months. Shortly after his return, he fractured a kneecap and missed the rest of the season. Broken fingers, sprained ankles, and a torn rotator cuff had become commonplace for Bryant. Some of his injuries required surgery, which took him out of the game he loved so much for extended

▶ BRYANT WAVES TO SPECTATORS DURING HIS LAST YEAR IN THE NBA.

▲ OVER THE YEARS, BRYANT HAD VARIOUS INJURIES THAT KEPT HIM OFF THE BASKETBALL COURT.

periods of time. The grueling level of competition that professional basketball demands combined with the standards that Bryant set for himself to remain at the top of the sport were wearing on his body. After nearly two decades in the NBA, it was becoming apparent that he wasn't as durable as he used to be.

Bryant announced that the 2015–16 season would be his last in the NBA. While the decision to retire wasn't an easy one, he faced it with the same focused energy that he had given all his previous endeavors. He wasn't sad about what was ending; he was excited about the new opportunities that lay ahead of him.

Of course, family and close friends knew about the decision before Bryant made his official announcement. One of the people he chose to share the big news with early was Michael Jordan. Bryant had actually sought Jordan's advice on the matter while making up his mind. He wanted to know when Jordan knew for sure that it was time to walk away from the game himself. As he had always done before, Jordan guided Bryant the best he could, telling him simply to enjoy his remaining time in the NBA.

THE PLAYER AND THE POET

Bryant had always stood out in the world of basketball as an exceptional player, but as he neared the end of his illustrious professional career in the sport, he also singled himself out with the way

Exclusively a Laker

When Bryant was drafted into the NBA, he became a Los Angeles Laker by chance, but he remained with the iconic Southern California team for the next 20 years largely by choice. The young boy who had attended Lakers games and told grown-ups that he wanted to play for the team one day himself had fulfilled that childhood dream, and he remained dedicated to the team for two long decades. In an era of trades and free agents who follow the best paycheck, Bryant stayed focused on earning championships for the team that took a chance on him all those years earlier. He ended his career as he'd begun it—wearing purple and gold.

he told his fans of his plans to leave the game. He chose to share his feelings about the sport and his decision to move on through a poem he titled "Dear Basketball." He posted the piece, a moving tribute to the game itself, on the *Players' Tribune* website in November 2015. In it, he told basketball, "I can't love you obsessively for much longer," and, "This season is all I have left to give."[1] When news of the poem broke, fans flocked to the site. The immense internet traffic crashed the website.

After releasing the poem, Bryant sent a copy to Jeanne Mastriano, his former high school English teacher. Along with Jordan, she too

From NBA Star to Oscar Winner

Bryant's fans embraced his "Dear Basketball" poem so deeply that Bryant decided to turn it into a short film following his retirement. Bryant narrated the film, Glen Keane animated and directed, and John Williams composed the music. Both Keane and Williams were big names in the entertainment industry. Keane was a leading animator for Disney, while Williams had written music for the legendary Star Wars movie series. The result of their collaboration with Bryant was a touching story of a boy who wanted nothing more than to become a professional basketball player—and who got to live his dream. The *Dear Basketball* film won an Oscar in 2018 for Best Animated Short, adding an unexpected award to Bryant's long list of basketball honors. When Keane accepted the Academy Award, he seemed to be talking about Bryant as much as the film. "It's through passion and perseverance that the impossible is possible," he told the audience.[2]

had been among those who knew the announcement was coming. Bryant had confided the news to her while he was still considering when he should tell the rest of the world. Part of him wanted to wait until he had played his last game. He told Mastriano that he was worried that there would be too much attention if everyone knew it was his last season. He didn't want standing ovations to detract from the games, but she urged him to tell his fans ahead of time, assuring him that they would want the opportunity to say goodbye to their hero.

Mastriano and many others loved the poem, even if it meant that their hero was nearing the end of his time on the court. The piece was essentially a love letter to basketball. It spoke of how the game had given a six-year-old boy his dream of playing the sport professionally. It was Bryant's way of thanking the game for all it had given him in exchange for his own hard work and devotion.

Making Wishes Come True

Bryant believed deeply in giving back to his community. One of his favorite charities was the Make-A-Wish Foundation, an organization that grants the wishes of critically ill children. When asked to name their biggest dream, many Make-A-Wish kids just want to meet their sports heroes, something Bryant made happen as often as he could. In donating his time to the foundation over the years, Bryant granted more than 200 wishes for sick children.[3]

BRYANT'S FAREWELL TOUR

Bryant's fans began referring to the 2015–16 NBA season as Bryant's Farewell Tour because of the tributes that started pouring in shortly after he announced his upcoming retirement. Even other NBA teams got in on the action, making videos and sending gifts to celebrate Bryant's long and admirable career. Some of the gestures, like the one made by the Atlanta Hawks, were rather creative. The team asked Zoo Atlanta to rename its resident black mamba snake, which now officially goes by the name of Kobe. Even the Boston Celtics, one of the Lakers' biggest rivals, presented Bryant with a gift, a piece of the famous parquet floor from their home court. The floor, which was used for 53 years of the team's history, was replaced in 1999. To receive a piece of it from the team was a high honor indeed.

Bryant's final season was not one for the record books, but he gave his fans a few special gifts of his own along the way. After playing a game in Denver, Bryant took off

A Double Honor

In a 2017 ceremony, the Los Angeles Lakers honored Bryant by retiring both of the player's former jersey numbers—8 and 24—with the team. It isn't unusual to set aside the number of a successful team member, but this was the first time the Lakers or any other team had retired two numbers worn by the same person. Bryant remains the only player to have two numbers retired by a single NBA team.

▲ BRYANT RECEIVED MANY TRIBUTES THAT CELEBRATED HIS BASKETBALL PROWESS EVEN AFTER HIS DEATH.

▲ Bryant steps on the court for the last basketball game of his career.

his sneakers and signed them for two boys who had come to see the game. He told the media that he hoped small gifts like this would leave his fans with a smile and a nice memory of him. He also frequently tossed his shooting sleeve into the crowd after a game.

Bryant played his last game in the NBA on April 13, 2016, against the Utah Jazz, which seemed fitting after his career-changing loss to the Salt Lake City team so many years earlier. He sank 22 shots on this final evening. Afterwards, he joked that for his entire career, people had been telling him that he didn't pass the ball enough—but that night all his teammates were urging him *not* to pass it for once. Bryant ended the game with 60 points, the sixth time in his career he'd scored at least 60 in a game. The Lakers won the game 101–96, but by its end they'd lost the magnificent player who had been the team's driving force for two decades.

9

A LIFE
WELL LIVED

Bryant's retirement offered him something that had been in short supply in his life for many years: free time. He spent most of it with the people he loved most, his wife and daughters. He was now able to be more involved in the day-to-day lives of Vanessa and their girls. He joked that after spending so much time traveling from city to city to play basketball, he was now on the road virtually all the time again, this time chauffeuring his daughters to school and their extracurricular activities.

▶ BRYANT AND GIANNA BOTH SHARED A LOVE OF BASKETBALL.

▲ THE BRYANT FAMILY ATTENDED A MOVIE PREMIERE
TOGETHER IN 2018.

He also fell in love with basketball all over
again, largely because of Gianna's intensifying
passion for the sport. The two were often spotted
at NBA and college games, discussing the plays
and cheering on the players. But this was a Bryant
the world hadn't seen when he wore a uniform.
The Black Mamba was gone, replaced by a father

nurturing his daughter's interests and talents. He also acted differently when he served as a coach for Gianna's middle school team. He served his new role with the calmness and maturity the position demanded. He seemed satisfied to be out of the spotlight. He focused on his children and their dreams.

The media would frequently ask Bryant whether he and his wife wished they had a son. The question seemed to imply that a daughter could not carry on his basketball legacy. During an appearance on *Jimmy Kimmel Live*, Bryant shared that this presumption annoyed Gianna. She saw herself the same way her parents did: completely capable of fulfilling her own dream of a professional basketball career. She hoped to play for the powerful University of Connecticut women's basketball program before launching a career in the WNBA.

Best Memories

Bryant had amassed a wealth of exciting experiences from his NBA career, but his favorite memories seemed to be of time he spent with his family. While discussing children with *Washington Post* reporter Kent Babb, Bryant said that one of the things he missed most was when his oldest daughter was a baby. When Natalia couldn't sleep in the middle of the night, he would get up and just hold her for hours. Despite all his fame and professional success, it was this type of memory that meant the most to him.

Bryant was proud of his daughters and was delighted to be their father. During an interview with ESPN's Elle Duncan, he declared, "Girls are the best. I would have five more girls if I could. I'm a girl dad."[1]

HELPING OTHERS EXCEL

In 2018, Bryant decided he wanted to do more for young athletes like Gianna. He founded a training facility called the Mamba Sports Academy in Thousand Oaks, California, for this purpose. He hired expert trainers, coaches, and physicians to work with aspiring athletes. In addition to basketball, the expansive facility helps athletes develop their skills in baseball, volleyball, and even jujitsu—a martial art.

Bryant continued to enjoy being part of the sport that had shaped his life so much, but from a vastly different perspective. Now, he watched as Gianna and the other kids who played basketball at the Mamba Sports Academy took

Sharing His Knowledge

Bryant held camps at his Mamba Sports Academy for professional athletes interested in learning even more about their chosen sports. In addition to the experts he employed, he also hosted workouts and tutorials personally. Bryant wanted to share things that he had learned about both the mental and physical parts of succeeding on the basketball court. His new goal, which he treated as seriously as his own ambitions in basketball, was to help others achieve their dreams on the court.

▲ AFTER BRYANT'S DEATH, THE MAMBA SPORTS ACADEMY CHANGED ITS NAME TO JUST THE SPORTS ACADEMY OUT OF RESPECT FOR THE BASKETBALL LEGEND.

the court. He was so proud of all of them that he said it was difficult to watch them play against one another at times.

Bryant had started traveling around Los Angeles by helicopter back when he was still playing for the Lakers. His demanding schedule kept him from being at home as often as he would have liked, and transportation only compounded the problem. One day he missed a school play that one of his daughters was in because he was stuck in heavy traffic. Now, he was utilizing helicopters to travel back and forth to the Mamba Sports Academy for similar reasons. This quicker form of transportation allowed him to spend more time with the whole family.

On Sunday, January 26, 2020, Bryant and Gianna boarded a helicopter to attend a basketball tournament at the academy. The father and daughter had invited six other people who were also heading to the event to travel with them that day—13-year-old Payton Chester and

#GirlDad

When ESPN reporter Elle Duncan heard the news of the helicopter crash, she was struck by the memory of Bryant telling her how much he enjoyed being a father to his daughters, how he'd proudly called himself a "girl dad" in her interview with him.[2] The following night, on *SportsCenter*, she told the story of how Bryant cherished his role as a father to girls, mentioning the phrase he'd used. His many fans who were also fathers to girls immediately took to social media using the hashtag #GirlDad as a way to honor both him and the important job of raising daughters. These men had been so inspired by Bryant's love and pride for his girls that they wanted to share with others how meaningful the sentiment was to them. #GirlDad became the top trending topic on Twitter, with the hashtag also included in almost 94,000 posts to Instagram.[3]

her mother, Sarah; 14-year-old Alyssa Altobelli and her parents, John and Keri; and the girls' coach, Christina Mauser. About 30 miles (48 km) west of downtown Los Angeles, something went terribly wrong. The helicopter, piloted by Ara Zobayan, crashed. The tragic accident took the lives of all nine people on board.

REACTIONS TO BRYANT'S DEATH

People around the world were stunned as news of the helicopter crash broke on television, radio, and the internet. Condolences and tributes for the 41-year-old basketball legend started pouring in immediately. An overwhelming number of Bryant's fans, friends, and fellow athletes turned to social media, trying to make sense of his unexpected passing. Many of them were in disbelief. "Please don't tell me this is true," tweeted one user. "This can't be real," wrote another. One person said simply, "Not Kobe."[4]

In the days and weeks following the crash, the tremendous outpouring of support from Bryant's

Shaq's Words

One of the people who spoke at Bryant and Gianna's public memorial service was Shaq. He said how proud he was of the three championships they won together for the Lakers, and he promised to teach Natalia, Bianka, and Capri how to do Bryant's basketball moves. He also spoke of how much he would miss the fellow player and rival who over time became a true friend. "Mamba," he said, "you were taken away from us way too soon. Your next chapter of life is just beginning. It's time for us to continue your legacy."[5]

fans and friends became a source of comfort for Vanessa and the couple's three surviving daughters. On February 24, 2020, around 20,000 people gathered at a memorial for Bryant and Gianna at the Staples Center in Los Angeles.[6] That was the same arena where Bryant had played so many games for the Lakers. Among the attendees were Kareem Abdul-Jabbar, Magic Johnson, Michael Jordan, Shaquille O'Neal, and dozens of other former and current NBA players. They all showed up to celebrate Bryant's life and grieve his passing along with his family.

Vanessa delivered the eulogies for her late husband and daughter. She spoke proudly of their individual personalities and the many traits the father and daughter shared. Vanessa and Bryant had spent the past 20 years as a family, a team of their own. Toward the end of her speech, she directed her words to Bryant. "Babe, you take care of our Gigi," she said through tears. "I got Nani, BiBi, and KoKo, and we're still the best team."[7]

Bryant's death marked the passing of one of the greatest basketball players of all time.

Hall of Fame

After Bryant's death, he was chosen to join other basketball greats in the Basketball Hall of Fame. "It's an incredible accomplishment and honor," said Vanessa. "We're extremely proud of him. Obviously, we wish he was here with us to celebrate."[8]

▲ TENS OF THOUSANDS OF SHIRTS WITH BRYANT'S JERSEY NUMBER WERE LAID OUT AT THE MEMORIAL SERVICE. TWO SEATS WERE DRAPED WITH BRYANT'S AND GIANNA'S JERSEYS.

His natural talent for the game, his enormous drive to push his abilities to their limits, and his generosity in nurturing the hopes and dreams of other athletes will never be forgotten. As Jordan said when he spoke at Bryant's memorial, "In the game of basketball, in life, as a parent—Kobe left nothing in the tank. He left it all on the floor."[9]

TIMELINE

1978

Kobe Bean Bryant is born on August 23 in Philadelphia, Pennsylvania.

1996

On June 26, the Charlotte Hornets select Bryant with the thirteenth pick in the NBA Draft.

1996

Bryant is traded to the Los Angeles Lakers within days of the June 26 draft.

2002

In February, Bryant is named All-Star MVP for the first of four times during his career.

2002

In June, Bryant and the Lakers win the NBA championship for a third year in a row.

2003

On January 19, Bryant's oldest daughter, Natalia, is born.

1997

Bryant is named to the NBA All-Rookie Second Team.

2000

Bryant and the Lakers defeat the Indiana Pacers to win the franchise's first NBA championship in 12 years.

2001

Bryant marries Vanessa Laine; he and the Lakers win the NBA championship again.

2006

On January 22, Bryant scores a career-high 81 points in a game against the Toronto Raptors.

2006

On May 1, Bryant's daughter Gianna is born.

2008

Bryant wins the NBA regular-season MVP award; he also wins his first Olympic gold medal at the Summer Games in Beijing.

TIMELINE

2009

Bryant adds a fourth NBA championship, his first without Shaquille O'Neal, to his long list of accomplishments with the Lakers.

2010

In February, Bryant breaks Jerry West's all-time scoring record for a Lakers player.

2010

In June, Bryant wins his fifth NBA championship with the Lakers when they defeat the rival Boston Celtics.

2016

On April 13, Bryant plays his last game before retiring from the NBA.

2016

On December 5, Bryant's daughter Bianka is born.

2018

The short film *Dear Basketball*, based on the poem Bryant wrote to announce his retirement from the NBA, wins an Academy Award.

2012

Bryant wins his second Olympic gold medal in London.

2014

Bryant passes Michael Jordan on the NBA's all-time scoring list.

2015

In November, Bryant announces that the 2015–16 NBA season will be his last.

2019

Bryant's youngest daughter, Capri, is born.

2020

On January 26, Bryant dies in a helicopter crash with his daughter Gianna and seven others.

2020

On February 24, thousands of people attend Bryant and Gianna's memorial service.

ESSENTIAL FACTS

DATE OF BIRTH

August 23, 1978

PLACE OF BIRTH

Philadelphia, Pennsylvania

PARENTS

Joe and Pamela Bryant

EDUCATION

Graduated from Lower Merion High School in 1996

MARRIAGE

April 18, 2001 to Vanessa Laine

CHILDREN

Natalia, Gianna, Bianka, and Capri

CAREER HIGHLIGHTS

Bryant rose to athletic stardom when he was drafted into the National Basketball Association (NBA) straight out of high school. As a career-long Lakers player, he led the team to five NBA championships. He also collected an impressive number of awards, including most valuable player (MVP) titles, along the way. Bryant won two Olympic gold medals with Team USA and even an Academy Award for a short film based on his original poem "Dear Basketball."

SOCIETAL CONTRIBUTION

Following his retirement, Bryant opened the Mamba Sports Academy. The facility focuses on training athletes of all ages to become the best versions of themselves in their respective sports. Bryant also became a champion for women's basketball at all levels.

CONFLICTS

The media often focused on Bryant's competitive challenges with fellow Lakers player Shaq. The two men had a complicated relationship, but they learned to work together long enough to bring home three of the five championship titles that Bryant won during his time with the Lakers. Another challenge that put Bryant in the spotlight off the basketball court was the charge of criminal sexual assault he faced in 2003. That charge was dropped a little over a year later.

QUOTE

"MVP nowadays is not an individual award. You really have to make your teammates better and elevate your ballclub. . . . From that standpoint, I feel like I've already won."

—Kobe Bryant after winning the MVP award for the
2007–08 season

GLOSSARY

assist
> A pass from one teammate to another that directly leads to a basket.

draft
> A process in which sports teams select the top eligible players to join them.

eulogy
> A personalized reading at a funeral to honor the deceased person.

mentor
> A person who teaches someone less experienced about a special skill.

postseason
> The playoff games that take place after the regular season.

power forward
> A basketball position given to a tall player with good rebounding skills.

rebound
> When a missed shot bounces off the rim or backboard and a player grabs it.

rookie
> An athlete in his or her first full season in a sport.

rotator cuff
> A part of the arm at the shoulder which allows range of motion.

shooting guard
> A basketball position whose main goals are scoring points and stealing the ball from the opposition.

shooting sleeve
> A cloth band that some basketball players wear on their arm, extending from wrist to bicep.

varsity
> The top-level team at a high school.

VHS tape
> A videocassette that contains magnetic tape with content recorded on it.

ADDITIONAL RESOURCES

SELECTED BIBLIOGRAPHY

Beacham, Greg. "12 Important Moments in Kobe Bryant's Remarkable Career." *AP News*, 12 Apr. 2016, apnews.com. Accessed 12 Mar. 2020.

Bose, Debanjali. "Inside Kobe and Shaq's Relationship: One of the NBA's Most Iconic Dynasties and Fiercest Rivalries." *Business Insider*, 31 Jan. 2020, businessinsider.com. Accessed 12 Mar. 2020.

Yaeger, Don. "Keep Shooting Your Shot: A Kobe Bryant Memory and a Lesson in Greatness." *Forbes*, 27 Jan. 2020, forbes.com. Accessed 12 Mar. 2020.

FURTHER READINGS

Bryant, Kobe. *The Mamba Mentality: How I Play*. Farrar, Strauss, and Giroux, 2018.

Graves, Will. *NBA*. Abdo, 2021.

Los Angeles Daily News. *Kobe: Forever*. Triumph Books, 2020.

ONLINE RESOURCES

To learn more about Kobe Bryant, please visit **abdobooklinks.com** or scan this QR code. These links are routinely monitored and updated to provide the most current information available.

MORE INFORMATION

For more information on this subject, contact or visit the following organizations:

Los Angeles Lakers
2275 E. Mariposa Ave.
El Segundo, CA 90245
310-426-6000
nba.com/lakers
The official Los Angeles Lakers website provides up-to-date information about the team and their schedule. People can also watch highlight videos, read about the team's history, and more.

Naismith Memorial Basketball Hall of Fame Museum
1000 Hall of Fame Ave.
Springfield, MA 01105
877-446-6752
hoophall.com
The Naismith Memorial Basketball Hall of Fame honors basketball's greats. This museum offers exhibits relating to the sport and hosts basketball shooting contests.

SOURCE NOTES

Chapter 1. A Career-Changing Game

1. Mark Medina. "Kobe Bryant's 'Airball Game' in 1997 Was [a] Defining Moment in His Career." *Los Angeles Daily News*, 15 Jan. 2016, dailynews.com. Accessed 12 May 2020.

2. Connor Friedersdorf. "Why Kobe Mourning Is So Intense." *Atlantic*, 29 Jan. 2020, theatlantic.com. Accessed 12 May 2020.

3. Medina, "Kobe Bryant's 'Airball Game.'"

4. Alicia Lee. "Why Kobe Bryant Gave Himself the Nickname 'Black Mamba.'" *CNN*, 27 Jan. 2020, cnn.com. Accessed 4 June 2020.

Chapter 2. Kobe's Younger Years

1. Claudio Lavanga. "A View of Kobe Bryant from His Childhood Home in Italy." *NBC News*, 27 Jan. 2020, nbcnews.com. Accessed 12 May 2020.

2. Lavanga, "A View of Kobe Bryant."

Chapter 3. Back in the USA

None.

Chapter 4. Going Pro

1. "Wilt Chamberlain." *Encyclopedia Britannica*, 27 Mar. 2020, britannica.com. Accessed 12 May 2020.

2. Marty Fenn. "Lakers Legend Kobe Bryant Initially Regretted Decision to Enter NBA out of High School." *Clutch Points*, 11 Jan. 2020, clutchpoints.com. Accessed 12 May 2020.

3. David Wharton et al. "Kobe Bryant's Devotion to Family Became Paramount When His Basketball Career Ended." *Los Angeles Times*, 28 Jan. 2020, latimes.com. Accessed 12 May 2020.

Chapter 5. Early Challenges, Fame, and Family

1. Jason Duane Hahn. "Kobe Bryant Opened Up about Meeting Wife Vanessa Bryant on 1999 Music Video Set in Documentary." *People*, 4 Feb. 2020, people.com. Accessed 12 May 2020.

2. Christine-Marie Liwag Dixon. "Kobe Bryant's Daughters: 5 Things You May Not Know." *List*, 29 Jan. 2020, thelist.com. Accessed 12 May 2020.

Chapter 6. A Career to Be Proud Of

1. "The 81-Point Game." *JR. NBA*, n.d., jr.nba.com. Accessed 12 May 2020.

Chapter 7. MVP Awards and Gold Medals

1. "Legends Profile: Magic Johnson." *NBA*, n.d., nba.com. Accessed 12 May 2020.

2. Larry Schwartz. "Kareem Wins a Record 6th NBA MVP Award." *ESPN Classic*, 19 Nov. 2003, espn.com. Accessed 12 May 2020.

3. "2007–08 NBA Awards Voting." *Basketball Reference*, n.d., basketball-reference.com. Accessed 12 May 2020.

4. Mike Bresnahan. "Bryant's 'M-V-P' Chants Come True." *Los Angeles Times*, 3 May 2008, latimes.com. Accessed 12 May 2020.

5. Andrew Binner. "What the Olympics Meant to Kobe Bryant." *Olympic Channel*, 27 Jan. 2020, olympicchannel.com. Accessed 12 May 2020.

6. "Kobe Bryant Becomes Lakers All-Time Leading Scorer." *NBA*, 1 Feb. 2010, nba.com. Accessed 12 May 2020.

SOURCE NOTES
CONTINUED

7. Tyler Conway. "Kobe Bryant Passes Michael Jordan on NBA's All-Time Scoring List." *Bleacher Report*, 14 Dec. 2014, bleacherreport.com. Accessed 12 May 2020.

Chapter 8. An Ending and a New Beginning
1. "Kobe Bryant to Retire after This Season." *ESPN*, 29 Nov. 2015, espn.com. Accessed 12 May 2020.
2. Klaritza Rico. "Kobe Bryant's 'Dear Basketball' Is Now Available to Watch for Free." *Variety*, 27 Jan. 2020, variety.com. Accessed 12 May 2020.
3. Jason Duaine Hahn. "Kobe Bryant Granted Over 200 Make-A-Wish Requests During Career; 'It Was the Highlight of My Life.'" *People*, 29 Jan. 2020, people.com. Accessed 12 May 2020.

Chapter 9. A Life Well Lived
1. Anna Hodges. "Kobe Bryant: What It Means to Be a #GirlDad." *BBC*, 30 Jan. 2020, bbc.com. Accessed 12 May 2020.
2. Angeline Jane Bernabe. "'Girl Dad' Goes Viral on Social Media after Sports Anchor Shares Heartfelt Story of Kobe Bryant." *Good Morning America*, 28 Jan. 2020, goodmorningamerica.com. Accessed 12 May 2020.
3. Bernabe, "'Girl Dad' Goes Viral."
4. "Sports World in Shock, Disbelief to Learn News of Kobe Bryant's Death." *NBC Sports*, 26 Jan. 2020, nbcsports.com. Accessed 12 May 2020.
5. Avery Yang. "Shaquille O'Neal Honors Kobe Bryant at Memorial: 'Kobe, You're Heaven's MVP.'" *Sports Illustrated*, 24 Feb. 2020, si.com. Accessed 12 May 2020.

6. "Public Memorial Service Remembers the Private Kobe Bryant." *USA Today*, 24 Feb. 2020, usatoday.com. Accessed 12 May 2020.

7. Scottie Andrew. "Read Vanessa Bryant's Speech at the Memorial for Kobe and Gigi Bryant." *CNN*, 24 Feb. 2020, cnn.com. Accessed 12 May 2020.

8. Wayne Sterling and Jay Croft. "Kobe Bryant Headlines Hall of Fame Class." *CNN*, 4 Apr. 2020, cnn.com. Accessed 12 May 2020.

9. Heather Tucker. "Michael Jordan Remembers His 'Little Brother' Kobe Bryant. Read His Entire Speech." *USA Today*, 24 Feb. 2020, usatoday.com. Accessed 12 May 2020.

INDEX

ABOUT THE AUTHOR

Tammy Gagne has written dozens of books for both adults and children. She lives in northern New England with her husband, son, and a menagerie of pets.